BRAZIL AND RIO DE JANEIRO

LOUISE SPILSBURY

W

FRANKLIN WATTS
LONDON•SYDNEY

BRAZIL AND RIO DE JANEIRO

FRANKLIN WATTS
LONDON•SYDNEY

First published in 2013 by
Franklin Watts
338 Euston Road
London
NW1 3BH

Franklin Watts Australia
Level 17/207 Kent Street
Sydney
NSW 2000

HB ISBN 978 1 4451 2361 5
Library eBook ISBN 978 14451 2367 7

Dewey number: 981'.066

A CIP catalogue record for this book is
available from the British Library.

Series Editor: Julia Bird
Series Advisor: Emma Epsley, geography teacher and consultant
Series Design: sprout.uk.com

Picture credits:
AF Archive/Alamy: 31b. Agenciaideal.com.br: 29b. Joedson Alves/dpa/Corbis: 18.
Anderdon/Dreamstime: 25. Andre Baertschi/NHPA/Photoshot: 41t. casadaphoto/Shutterstock: 9bl. Carlos Cazalis/Corbis:
24t. Marcia Chambers/Alamy: 20. Andre M Chang/Alamy: 22. Yasuyoshi Chiba/AFP/Getty Images: 14. Copperman05/
Dreamstime:33. Neal Cousland/ Shutterstock: 8b. Djembe/Dreamstime: 27tl. ecoventurestravel/Shutterstock: 40. eky studio/
Shutterstock:9tl. David Evans/NG/Alamy: 21. fotoember/istockphoto: 38. David R Frazier/Alamy: 29t. Front page/Shutterstock:
8t, 41b. JBK/Shutterstock: 24b. Vitoriano Junior/Shutterstock: 16b. Art Kowalsky/Alamy: 17t. Yadid Levy/Alamy: front cover t,
3t, 11bl. Carlos Mora/Dreamstime: 43. Sergio Moraes/Reuters/Corbis: 36. Roberto Tetsuo Okamura/Shutterstock: 6b. Gianni
Dagli Orti/Art Archive/Alamy: 12. Gigi Peis/Shutterstock: 31t. Peterv/istockphoto: 13t. Pers Anders Pettersson/Corbis: 28.
photofriday/Shutterstock: 35b. Picturepoint/Topham: 11t. Pietrack/Dreamstime: 27b. pukach/Shutterstock: 9br. Celso Pupo/
Shutterstock: 11br, 27tr.. Luiz Rocha/Shutterstock: 30. Marcelo Sayo/epa/Alamy: 19. Keith Sherwood/Shutterstock: 15t.
Skynavin/Shutterstock: 9tr. Jan Sochor/Alamy: 32. Peter Stoh/Alamy: 39. Mark Swettmann/Shutterstock: 17br. Marcelo Tasso/
Agencia Estado/Photoshot: 23. Luis Carlos Torres/istockphoto: 17bl. Peter Treanor/Alamy; 26b, 35t. Marc Turcan/Shutterstock:
front cover b, 3b, 10t. Vanderleialmedia/AFP/Getty Images: 34. John van Hasselt/Corbis: 42.

Printed in Malaysia

Franklin Watts is a division of
Hachette Children's Books,
an Hachette UK company.
www.hachette.co.uk

DEVELOPING
WORLD

BRAZIL AND RIO DE JANEIRO

CONTENTS

CHANGING TIMES

The name Brazil conjures up images of football, carnival, beautiful beaches and the Amazon rainforest. But Brazil is much more. Its landscapes include grassland, desert and wetlands. Its citizens range from indigenous tribespeople who spend their lives deep in the rainforest, to jetsetting billionaires. Brazil is also the fifth largest country in the world, and has one of the fastest growing economies.

ECONOMIC POWERHOUSE

Brazil has undergone a period of rapid economic growth in its recent history. It is the largest economy in the whole of South America, making it the continent's most influential country. Brazil is also a rising economic power on the world stage, ranking as the eighth largest economy in the world, just behind the USA, Japan and Germany but ahead of the UK, France, Italy and many other more developed countries. With increasing earnings from industry and high employment, the Brazilian people are on average getting richer and consuming more goods and services. The government is responding by investing more in Brazil's infrastructure, such as roads and electricity supply.

The Brazilian Pantanal, or wetlands, sprawl across the western states of Mato Grosso do Sul and Mato Grosso, covering an area of around 150,000 square kilometres.

VENEZUELA
GUYANA
FRENCH
GUIANA
COLOMBIA
SURINAME

EQUATOR

Manaus

The Amazon

Fortaleza

Natal
Recife

PERU

BRAZIL

Salvador

Brasília

BOLIVIA
The Pantanal

Paraná River

CHILE
PARAGUAY

Rio de Janeiro
São Paulo

IGUAÇU FALLS

Pacific Ocean

Atlantic Ocean

ARGENTINA

Porto Alegre

URUGUAY

CENTRES OF GROWTH

Today, Brazil's capital city is Brasília, one of the world's newest cities, completed in 1960. Brazil's capital was rebuilt partly because the original capital, Rio de Janeiro, was overcrowded. Relocating the capital also brought it to a more central location in the country.

However, Rio remains the most visited city in the southern hemisphere. It has a thriving industrial and financial centre and is a regional media and communications hub. The majority of Brazil's industries have their base here and it boasts many of their best universities. But the city faces many challenges confronting the country as a whole, such as balancing the needs of the growing richer middle classes with the poor, and balancing economic development with protection of the environment.

SPOTLIGHT ON BRAZIL

SIZE: 8,511,965 km² • COASTLINE: 7,367 km
MAJOR RIVER: Amazon (3,615 km) •
POPULATION: 192 million • MAJOR
LANGUAGE: Portuguese • MAJOR RELIGION:
Christianity • HEAD OF STATE: President Dilma
Rousseff • MAIN EXPORTS: cars, aircraft, steel,
coffee, footwear, soya beans

DIVERSE LANDSCAPE

LAND AND SETTLEMENTS

Brazil is a country of diverse regions, with a rich range of natural resources and major settlements that were often based around these. Many places were first founded by European settlers in the country, in particular the Portuguese who colonised the country from the 16th until the 19th centuries. For example, Salvador in the South East region was established as a port in 1549 by the Portuguese to export sugar to Europe from plantations. It was also the port into which they imported African slaves to work on plantations from the 17th century onwards (see page 10). Manaus in the North region developed in the late 19th century after demand grew around the world for rubber from rainforest trees to make tyres and other objects. Manaus lies on a tributary of the Amazon River and rubber could be easily transported from here by boat to the Atlantic. From there, it was shipped to ports all over the world.

WEST CENTRAL

AREA: 19% of Brazil

POPULATION: 7% of Brazilian total

DENSITY: 9 people per km^2

MAJOR LANDSCAPE: savanna and tropical grassland; Pantanal wetland

CLIMATE: warm subtropical

MAJOR CITIES: Brasília

ECONOMY: agriculture (including cattle breeding), mining

WATER FEATURES

In the South are two of Brazil's most amazing water features. The majestic Iguaçu Falls are made up of 275 individual falls where the Paraná River cascades over a plateau around 80m high. This rushing water has been put to good use at Itaipu, where there is the biggest hydroelectric dam in the world, creating enormous amounts of power.

NORTH

AREA: 46% of Brazil

POPULATION: 8% of Brazilian total

DENSITY: 4 people per km^2

MAJOR LANDSCAPE: Amazon rainforest

CLIMATE: warm and moist most of year with 2 metres annual rainfall

MAJOR CITIES: Manaus

ECONOMY: forest products, electronics

NORTH EAST

AREA: 18% of Brazil

POPULATION: 28% of Brazilian total

DENSITY: 34 people per km^2

MAJOR LANDSCAPE: caatinga (scrubby desert)

CLIMATE: hot, dry summers, with frequent droughts

MAJOR CITIES: Salvador, Fortaleza

ECONOMY: agriculture (including sugar cane), shipping, oil

SOUTH

AREA: 7% of Brazil

POPULATION: 14% of Brazilian total

DENSITY: 49 people per km^2

MAJOR LANDSCAPE: pampas grassland

CLIMATE: damp summers and dry, cold winters

MAJOR CITIES: Porto Alegre

ECONOMY: agriculture and manufacturing

SOUTH EAST

AREA: 11% of Brazil

POPULATION: 42% of Brazilian total

DENSITY: 87 people per km^2

MAJOR LANDSCAPE: Atlantic rainforest

CLIMATE: warm, temperate with regular rainy seasons

MAJOR CITIES: São Paulo, Rio de Janeiro

ECONOMY: services, manufacturing, minerals, agriculture (including coffee and animal products)

9

FOCUS ON: RIO

RIO DE JANEIRO

In early 1502, Portuguese sailors reaching South America discovered a sheltered natural bay on the Atlantic coast. They thought at first it was the mouth of a river they could follow into the interior of the continent. But even though there was no river they set up a colony there, attracted by its beauty and warm climate. They named the place Rio (river) de Janeiro (January, the month of discovery). The settlement remained small until a conflict with French traders over timber extraction from the surrounding forests. After defeating the French, settlers started to farm the surrounding area and the city of São Sebastião do Rio de Janeiro began to grow.

MINERAL WEALTH

At the start of the 18th century, miners discovered gold and diamonds in the nearby region of Minas Gerais. Rio became established as the main trading port for these valuable exports, and its population grew rapidly. In 1763 the Portuguese moved their capital from the port of Salvador in Bahia to Rio, and Rio remained the capital when Brazil became independent from Portugal in 1822. By the late 19th century, Rio was one of the biggest cities in the world with half a million inhabitants or *cariocas*. It has continued to grow steadily since then, with a population today of over 6.3 million.

Portuguese explorers began to settle in Rio in the early 16th century.

SPRAWLING CITY

As Rio has developed and grown, it has needed more space for buildings and people. One solution has been major engineering projects that have removed surrounding mountains and filled in parts of the bay to create land. Others include building high-rise housing and skyscrapers to fit more people on less land, and merging with surrounding small settlements such as Niteroi and Nova Iguaçu. Today Rio is a vast, sprawling city made up of several zones. The south zone is the coastal strip, boasting the famous beaches of Copacabana and Ipanema. A mountain range including the famous Sugar Loaf Mountain separates this from the centre and north zones where most of Rio's housing and industry are located. Extensive roads, mountain tunnels and a subway link the zones together.

The famous statue of Christ the Redeemer, at the summit of Corcovado mountain, overlooks the city and bay of Rio.

Its colonial past and centuries of immigration mean that Rio has a richly diverse population.

The famous beaches of Rio attract tourists from all over the world.

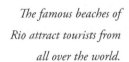

11

PAST TO PRESENT

Atlas

Lith 2.

SETTLERS

Before the arrival of the Portuguese settlers, Brazil's population was entirely made up of indigenous peoples. There were hundreds of individual tribes, such as the Guarani living near the coast and the Arawak and Yanomani further inland, each speaking different languages. The Portuguese connection transformed the country and has been largely responsible for the cultural mix, settlements and language in today's Brazil.

SLAVERY

From the 16th century onwards, waves of white Portuguese settlers reached Brazil. Portugal was a major player in the transatlantic slave trade, and the Portuguese colonists were able to obtain slaves from West Africa easily and cheaply. They set the slaves to work on Brazil's new sugar plantations, which were key to the country's rapidly growing economy. Between the 16th and 19th century, when slavery was finally made illegal, around five million black slaves were shipped over to work in Brazil.

This painting shows a slave in Rio de Janeiro in the 1830s. Brazil had the largest slave population in the world and more than 600,000 slaves passed through Rio in the early 19th century.

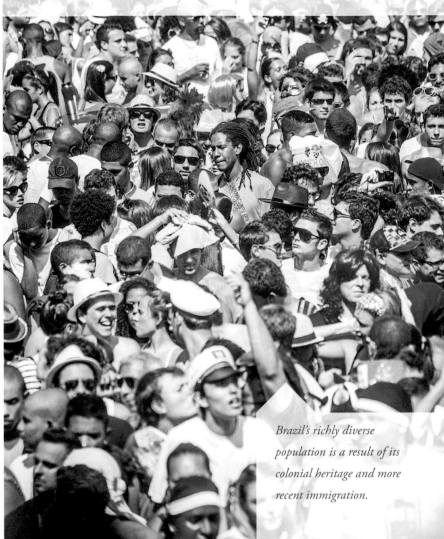

Brazil's richly diverse population is a result of its colonial heritage and more recent immigration.

A MIXED POPULATION

Over time, Brazilians from different ethnic backgrounds had children together, creating a large mixed-race population known as *mulatto* or *pardo* in Brazil. In the 19th century, following Brazil's independence, many thousands of other settlers arrived, including people from Germany, Italy and Japan, who were attracted by Brazil's land and economic opportunities. Today indigenous peoples are a minority in Brazil.

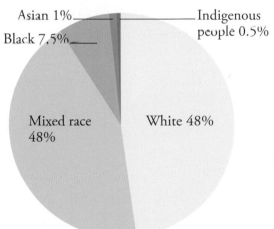

Asian 1%
Black 7.5%
Indigenous people 0.5%
Mixed race 48%
White 48%

RACIAL DEMOCRACY

Inequality still hampers Brazil's development. Income for white Brazilians is, on average, double what it is for black or mixed-race Brazilians. Black Brazilians in general have poorer education, living conditions and access to healthcare than whites. It takes a long time for attitudes to change, but people are trying. Since 2001 20 per cent of places in Rio de Janeiro's state universities have been allocated to black students who pass the entrance exam. A further percentage of places are taken by people whose parents' income is very low.

LAND RIGHTS

The Yanomani are one of 220 tribes of Brazilian indigenous people. Around 20,000 Yanomani live in over 200 villages in the north of Brazil. In 1992 the Brazilian government designated certain areas of land for exclusive use by Yanomani to protect their land and homes. However, illegal gold mining and ranching has continued in these areas. The Yanomani and other tribes continue to lobby the government to protect their land and way of life. In 2013 their protests encouraged Brazilian authorities to evict illegal ranchers from their lands.

POPULATION SHIFTS

ON THE DECLINE

As Brazil develops economically, its population is growing at a slower rate. In the 1970s Brazilian families had an average of five children; today the average is just two. There are a number of reasons for this, including better access to family planning, more women working and the rising cost of raising and educating children as more Brazilians move to expensive urban areas. However, a large proportion of Brazilians are young. If many of these people have children, the population could increase faster again in future. This is in contrast to countries such as the UK where the average age is over 40, meaning most people are past child-bearing age.

URBAN MIGRATION

More and more people have moved to the cities as Brazil has developed. Most live in bigger cities such as Rio, São Paulo and Salvador along the coast, where there is generally more work. Many Brazilians now living in cities are migrants or descendants of migrants from rural areas inland. Most moved to urban areas for work, because they lost their jobs due to the mechanisation of Brazil's farms or enviromental problems. For example,

Women in Brazil are having fewer children and leaving it later in life to start a family.

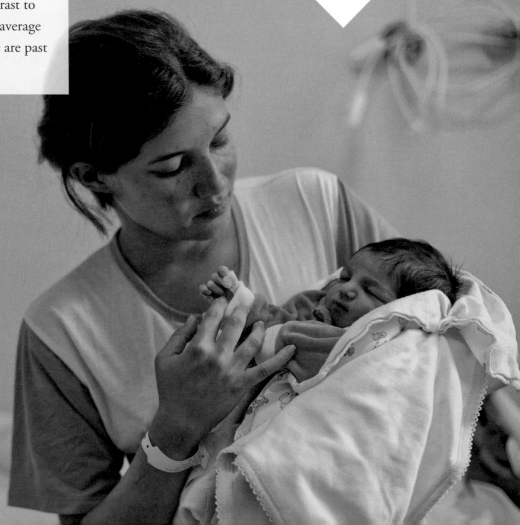

many people moved to Rio from the North East region after droughts during the 1950s ruined crops. City life can also often offer a higher standard of living and better infrastructure. Around 85 per cent of urban Brazilians have access to sanitation – the safe disposal of human waste – which is about twice the proportion (44 per cent) for rural dwellers.

HOMES AND HOUSES

Because of Brazil's recent economic development, the average Brazilian now lives in a house made from brick, stone or concrete, with access to electricity, the Internet and other amenities. However, some Brazilians still live in traditional wooden huts far from the electricity grid, some on stilts over the Amazon River and others in forest clearings. In big cities there is lots of modern housing, such as apartments in high-rise blocks or suburban homes with gardens, but these types of housing are inaccessible to many poorer urban Brazilians. When cities such as Rio grew quickly in the early to mid-20th century, the lack of affordable housing forced many people to take over land at the city edges and build their own low-cost homes. These settlements are known as *favelas* [see page 16].

Water levels in the Amazon can be very low some years, but swell to create floods in others. Houses along the river are built on stilts to hold them above the water.

POPULATION CHANGE SINCE 1775 (MILLIONS)

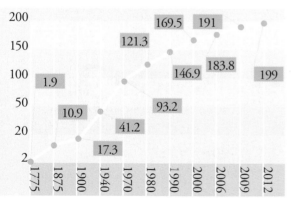

Brazil's rate of population growth was very high during the early and mid-20th century, but has slowed significantly since 1970.

FOCUS ON: RIO

LIVING IN RIO

Rio, like any big city around the world, is home to people with very different employment, incomes and homes. Around 20 per cent of its inhabitants – one million people – live in favelas and are known as *favelados*. There are around 1,000 of these shanty towns perched on the steep hillsides overlooking downtown Rio. Each favela has a different name. The biggest is called Rocinha.

A resident of Rocinha in 2012 recalls what life was like there as a child:
'We lived in a two-room [wooden] shack all six of us. The bathroom was outside and we had to shower outside in our underwear. A shower was two buckets of water, one to get wet and soap up, the other to clean off the soap. This was life and you get used to it. We had no electricity, just lamps and candles. We finally got a TV hookup when I was about 9. We had to run a wire from a neighbour's house to get power.'

FAVELAS TODAY

Today many favela homes are bigger, and made from stronger materials such as brick, concrete blocks or metal sheets. They often have electricity, piped water and sometimes an inside toilet. However, services such as waste collection and sanitation are poor because the government considers many favelados to be illegally occupying city land. Good healthcare is also not always available. Big favelas such as Rocinha have healthcare centres but many don't, and the favelados

suffer as a result. Infant mortality in a favela in Rio is three times greater than in the rich Rio suburb of Barra da Tijuca, for example. Favelas have a reputation for violence, crime and other social problems, yet they are also unique, close-knit communities where many people work together to try to improve their living conditions.

DIFFERENT LIVES

Some of the richest Rio residents live in high-rise apartments overlooking the famous Copacabana beach, shop at luxury stores and send their children to exclusive schools. But overcrowding, inflated property prices and city centre pollution are just a few reasons why some richer inhabitants have moved to affluent newer suburbs such as Barra da Tijuca. Barra is cleaner, less polluted and has wide avenues lined with big, gated homes. It has a big shopping mall, convention centre, theme parks and a cleaner beach than Copacabana. It also has a newly developing favela where construction workers and other less wealthy people working in Barra can live.

A favela perched on a steep slope in Rio de Janeiro.

A street in Rocinha favela in Rio. Between one to two hundred thousand people live in this densely populated favela, which dates back to the early 20th century.

High-rise apartments crowd along Rio's Barra da Tijuca shoreline.

Wealthier Rio residents live in large detached houses in the suburbs.

GOVERNING BRAZIL

Brazilian President Dilma Rousseff poses with US Secretary of State Hillary Clinton, after the presidential inauguration ceremony in January 2011.

POLITICAL PICTURE

The election of Dilma Rousseff as president in 2011 illustrates just how Brazil has changed in recent history. In the 1970s Brazil was a military dictatorship under which there was no freedom of speech, political parties were banned and many dissenters were tortured or killed. Today, it is a thriving democracy with fair elections and a female leader governing its 26 states.

FROM DEBT TO DEMOCRACY

During the late 1960s and early 1970s, Brazil's economy grew by about ten per cent each year, but only because military rulers borrowed from international banks. They undertook giant construction projects like the Transamazônica highway, which stretches from the coast to the rainforest. Without economic reform, however, debts

stacked up and by the late 1970s people were starving. Many protested, including Rousseff herself who was arrested and tortured, and military rule was over by the early 1980s. However, it wasn't until 2002 that real economic progress began. Under President Lula (2003–2011) the country repaid its US$15 billion debt to the International Monetary Fund (IMF). Inflation fell, the minimum wage was raised, and a monthly payment to poor families – the *Bolsa Familia* – helped to lift millions out of poverty.

CHALLENGES

Today Brazil is a democracy and four peaceful presidential elections have helped to build its reputation as a safe, strong country with which to do business. In 2012, Rousseff had an approval rating of 77 per cent, but her government still faces challenges. One is to keep Brazil's economy expanding, even though growth is showing signs of slowing down. The government is addressing this by investing more money in Brazil's key industries. Other ongoing aims are to invest more in the country's infrastructure, such as its roads, buildings and power supply. The government also targets helping people out of poverty and giving more young people the chance of reaching a high standard of education.

Brazilian army and military police at work patrolling the outskirts of a local favela.

POLICE AND MILITARY

One role of the Brazil government is to provide police and military forces. The federal police deal with border control, terrorism and issues affecting the country as a whole, whereas state police uphold local laws and investigate crimes in the state. All people aged 17–45 years must undergo nine to 12 months of military service in the army, navy or airforce. Brazil has the largest military force in South America at around half a million members. Its roles vary from jungle warfare to evacuating flood victims or keeping the peace in war zones.

EDUCATION

OFF TO SCHOOL

Today all children between seven and 14 in Brazil go to school, but in the past school attendance was low. Poor families cannot afford school meals and uniforms and may need to keep children at home to work. The Brazilian government improved basic education in different ways from the mid-1990s by investing in training and resources. It provided equipment and millions of schoolbooks, screened educational TV programmes and gave free school meals to poorer students to encourage families to send their children to school.

RICH V POOR

Standards vary widely in Brazil's schools. In richer areas, schools often have better facilities, higher standards of teacher training and smaller class sizes. This is especially the case at private schools where people pay for their children to attend. In remote or poor areas, large classes, poor facilities and poor attendance of teachers can negatively affect the quality of education offered. A comparison of education standards reached in Brazil and other countries revealed that Brazilian childrens' average performance in science, maths and reading was behind that of Chilean, Uruguayan and Argentinian children of the same age, and far behind that of children in most of Europe and Asia.

In rural areas some children have to walk several kilometres to reach their school.

A primary school class at work in Cachoeira, in the state of Bahia.

STUDYING FURTHER

Attending high school and university is free in Brazil. Most Brazilians enrol at high school but there is a high dropout rate, especially in rural areas where some young people prefer to earn money rather than study and where basic education has already been poor. Again the government has tried to encourage greater attendance, for example with the Family Grant scheme where families are paid state benefits only if their children carry on regularly attending school. As the country develops, the number of universities in Brazil is increasing, but only around 30 per cent of people of university age have sufficient qualifications to actually enrol. The issue for Brazil is that even while the country is developing, it is not currently producing enough educated young people and graduates to enhance its workforce, train the next generation of Brazilians and help the country realise its full economic potential. In Korea, for example, ten times the number of engineers graduate per thousand people than in Brazil.

Brazil hopes to get more students in to higher education to help the country develop further in the future.

CRIME

Military police and organised criminal gangs can be involved in violent clashes.

DANGEROUS AREAS

In 2012 shootouts between the police and criminal gangs in São Paulo killed over 1,000 people, including 94 police officers. No wonder that the United Nations has described some neighbourhoods in São Paulo as the most dangerous on Earth. One reason policing is failing in Brazil is that officers are poorly paid and may take bribes to turn a blind eye to the criminals. This is all the more likely if the officers grew up on the same streets as, and live alongside, the criminals.

POVERTY AND CRIME

Brazil's crime problem is linked with development. When people are poor and have limited opportunities, they may be more likely to turn to crime. The drug trade has been dominant in Rio's favelas since the 1980s when cocaine sellers started to recruit poor favelados to help sell the drug through the city. This drug trade has fuelled crime in and around the favelas, not only causing robberies to fund drug use, but also provoking violence in the form of armed battles between rival drug gangs and between drug gangs and the police. Dealing with crime uses money that could help the country develop. The Brazilian government spends around US$34 billion each year on public safety, prisons and treating victims of violence, but just US$30 billion on education.

TAKING ACTION

The Brazilian government is attempting to crack down on crime with better training and wages for police officers and firmer punishment for offenders. It is also reducing the availability of guns by making it illegal to carry firearms and offering cash to buy them from people. Educating people about crime is also a priority for the government. If young people learn about the dangers to themselves, their families and communities, they may be less likely to become criminals.

A Pacifying Police Unit (UPP) patrols the streets of the Rocinha favela in Rio.

POLICE PATROLS

Rio has a reputation for high crime rates, but authorities there are trying a new approach. Starting from 2008, officers from Pacifying Police Units (UPP) patrol the streets in the favelas. Their main priority is to reclaim the streets from armed gangs to make residents feel safer. They confiscate guns to get them off the streets, move on drug sellers, and encourage local people to anonymously report criminal activity to a government hotline. This community approach to policing has reduced the rate of murders in many favelas. It has also increased respect for the police amongst favelados.

'This is a new moment… the first time we have police here and the first time we can really say we have security.'

Raimundo Vilar de Oliveira, shopkeeper in a Rio favela

ECONOMIC POWERHOUSE

Embraer makes a wide range of aeroplanes, from luxury executive jets and small airliners to military training and crop spraying aeroplanes. It has 16 factories, training centres and offices in Brazil and five other countries.

BRIC POWER

Brazil, Russia, India, China and South Africa are sometimes grouped together as the BRICS nations because they are all developing countries with large, emerging economies. Together they make up nearly a sixth of the global economy. The economies of these five countries are growing faster than many others in the world, including those of more developed countries. This growing economic power gives the BRICS countries a strong presence in world trade.

COMMODITIES

Brazil is rich in natural resources and it relies on selling goods derived from these resources around the world. These include coffee, orange juice, sugar, soya beans, beef and leather products from cattle, and mined raw materials such as iron ore and oil. Brazil is currently the tenth biggest oil producer in the world. However, recent oil finds could help catapult Brazil into the top five producers by 2020. Brazil also exports products such as cars and planes. One of its major companies, Embraer (see above), is the third biggest aircraft maker in the world.

MORE WEALTH, MORE SPENDING

As Brazil has developed, more Brazilians have more money to spend. Today, over 100 million Brazilians work and just six per cent of people of working age are unemployed. In the past most people worked in agriculture, but today around two-thirds of people work in service industries, for example in shops, hotels and banks. The average wage of US$12,000 a year is less than that paid in more developed countries, but much greater than the average wage in its fellow BRICS economy, India. However, Brazil's economic growth is limited partly by a lack of skilled labour, as well as by a shortage of people educated at a higher level who can create new industries and enhance old ones. Further government investment in education should help to keep the economy developing.

NEW PARTNERSHIPS

In the past Brazil mostly exported and imported goods to and from more developed regions such as the USA, Japan and Europe. Today its major trade partner is China. China imports iron ore and oil to fuel its industries and provide power, and buys Brazilian foods such as soya beans. China is also investing money in Brazil. In 2010 China's largest machinery manufacturer, Sany, spent US$200 million on a new plant in São Paulo which produces construction machines. These machines will help build sites for the forthcoming Olympics and World Cup in Brazil (see pages 36–37). Brazil itself is investing in less developed countries. For example, Brazilian mining company Vale is developing coal mining in Mozambique.

Brazil's Pavilion at the world fair in Shanghai, China in 2010 was designed to look like a tropical forest.
It contained several exhibition halls to celebrate Brazil and to highlight its economic progress.

FOCUS ON: RIO

WORKING IN RIO

Rio de Janeiro has the second largest economy of any Brazilian city, after São Paulo, accounting for around seven per cent of the country's GDP. Rio is not only an economic hub for import and export of goods, with a major airport and port, but also has diverse industries manufacturing a wide range of products, including processed foods, medicines, textiles and products made from oil. The state oil company, Petrobras, has its headquarters in Rio. Following new oil discoveries and increased demand for fuels Petrobras has created thousands of jobs in and around the city. These range from welders of piping used in refineries to oil rig workers and brokers selling rights to drill oil in Brazilian territory to foreign companies.

SERVICES

Most workers in Rio de Janeiro have jobs providing services, such as selling goods, teaching and banking. Rio is one of the leading financial centres in the country, with headquarters of major banks such as Caixa Econômica Federal. It is home to major Brazilian media companies such as TV Globo and the headquarters of many international companies such as pharmaceutical giant Merck. The range of service jobs includes formal jobs which pay a regular monthly wage, such as teaching, and informal jobs where people's income depends entirely on demand for their services, such as a musician.

TOURISM

Tourists flock to Rio to see its sights. Each year around one million visitors fill up the hotels and hostels in town at carnival time. Jobs in tourism vary a lot. Some workers clean rooms, while others book rooms, or serve or cook in restaurants. Others sell goods such as pineapples, cold drinks, bikinis and flip-flops to tourists on the busy city beaches of Ipanema and Copacabana. Some people entertain or educate tourists. Samba performers run classes to teach drumming and dancing to visitors. Exotic tours hire locals to show tourists around their favelas.

WAGES IN RIO

Here are some examples of what workers in Rio earned in 2012:

JOB	ANNUAL WAGE
Samba drummer	£4,600
Refinery welder	£6,200
Beach vendor	£6,200
Doorman	£6,800
Flight attendant	£16,000

Samba is the national music of Brazil. Most tourists visiting Rio hope to see a Samba band in action.

Vendors sell to tourists and locals on the beach at Copacabana.

The headquarters of Brazilian oil and energy giant Petrobras.

The snacks sold at Rio's bustling street stalls reflect the city's history, ranging from indigenous dishes to snacks passed down from Portuguese and African settlers.

TRANSPORT AND COMMUNICATIONS

GETTING AROUND

Brazil is a huge country and travelling around it is slow because most transport is by road, as few railways are in working order. Motorways are limited and many other roads are unpaved or in a bad state of repair. Better transport links are essential for Brazil's development to enable workers and goods to move more quickly around the country. For example, to travel the 2,777 km from Manaus in the north to the city of Natal on the northeast coast can take a week by car, but just seven hours by aeroplane. The problem is that although more people can afford to fly, Brazil's airports cannot handle the increasing demand for flights. That is why a key focus of the government's programme of investment in infrastructure launched in 2007 is to improve roads, upgrade airports, improve Brazil's ports and fund a new high-speed train link between Rio and São Paulo.

Many of Brazil's roads are in poor condition and make driving around the country dangerous.

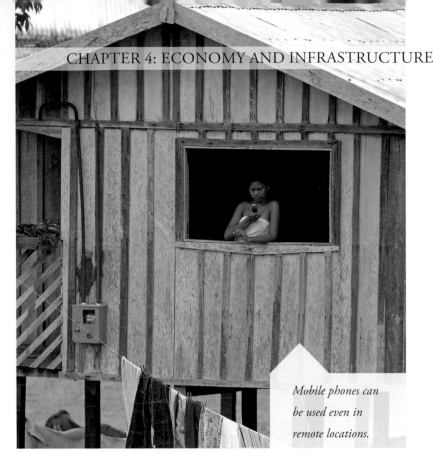

CONNECTIONS

People across Brazil use mobiles rather than landlines, partly because the wiring infrastructure is not sufficient across its vast area. Brazil is the fourth largest mobile phone market in the world, with over 260 million connections in 2012, nearly 1.5 times the total population. Mobile broadband use outstrips fixed Internet connections, too. In 2012 there were 60 million mobile broadband connections and this is predicted to rise by a quarter by 2016. Driving this demand is not only use of social media but also a host of services. These include mobile banking, e-payments and industry-specific services, such as insect pest recognition and advice on eradication for farmers. The government is making sure that mobiles continue to benefit the country's development by improving networks and encouraging manufacturers to produce cheaper smartphones.

Mobile phones can be used even in remote locations.

The Superporto do Açu shipping complex, north of Rio.

SUPER PORT

North of Rio de Janeiro is a giant pier jutting around four kilometres out to sea. This is part of the Superporto do Açu shipping complex which opens in 2013. The pier will make it easier for giant ships to dock, load and transport millions of tonnes of Brazilian commodities and products. The project is controversial, partly because its construction may be raising salt levels in nearby rivers and lakes, affecting drinking water and wildlife habitats, and partly because Chinese investment in the project gives them partial control over the port and its industries. Yet the Superporto will not only bring jobs to the region, it will also help promote Brazilian trade.

TOURISM

FUELLING THE ECONOMY

Travel and tourism is an important industry in Brazil, generating nearly nine per cent of the country's GDP. Tourism creates and supports jobs. When tourists visit a place they not only spend money on seeing particular attractions, they also support restaurants, shops and hotels, as well transport, banks and many other services.

Many tourists visit Brazil to enjoy its famous golden sands.

TOURISM RATES

Brazil had only around five million international tourist arrivals each year from 2005 to 2012, placing it well outside the top 10 global tourism destinations. Some visitors are put off by reports of crime and violence and many of those that do go to Brazil don't venture far from Rio, São Paulo and the Amazon. The Brazil government wants to develop the tourism industry in different regions by promoting their unique features. Bahia state in the Northeast for example has sandy beaches and clean seas, low rainfall, colonial heritage and cultural diversity. Other less-visited sites include Iguaçu Falls on the Argentinian border and the Pantanal, a vast wetland area in the South with remarkable biodiversity, ranging from capybaras to anacondas.

Tourists flock to the historic city of Ouro Preto in the state of Minas Gerais. It has beautiful churches, bridges and fountains dating from the 18th century when the area's gold mines made it rich.

The government trailed adverts for Brazil before the 3D animated film Rio. The film features a parrot flying over Brazil and highlighting its beauty and diversity.

CAMPAIGNS

In 2012 the government tourist board launched a giant campaign called 'The World Meets in Brazil, Come Celebrate Life' which involved exhibitions, brochures, posters and TV adverts shown around the world. The aim is to double foreign tourist arrivals each year by 2017 and to triple tourism income. Many tourists will be attracted by two global events hosted by Brazil, the 2014 FIFA World Cup and the 2016 Olympics. The government anticipates an extra 600,000 visitors for the World Cup alone. It is improving infrastructure for tourism so they enjoy a good experience for example by spending over £7 billion on improving airports, renovating hotels and training tourism staff at the World Cup host cities.

CHANGING CULTURE

LANGUAGE

Brazil's culture – its religion, art, music, and pastimes – is always evolving, as witnessed even by the language its people speak. Since the 16th century, the majority of Brazilians have spoken Portuguese as their first language, but their version differs greatly from that spoken in Portugal as it has developed to include words from the many languages spoken by Brazil's indigenous peoples and from other immigrants. For example, many people say 'tchau' to mean 'bye', which comes from the Italian 'ciao'. Names and terms for new foreign products and technologies are also being introduced as the country develops economically.

FAITH

The country's religious life is also changing. In 1980 nearly 90 per cent of the population was Roman Catholic; today that figure has dropped to under 70 per cent. As people earn more, are better educated, learn other languages and have more contact with foreign countries, some are re-evaluating old traditions and choosing other options. As numbers of Catholics are falling, there is a growing presence of modern Protestant denominations such as Evangelical and Pentecostal, more interest in traditional religions such as Candomblé (see panel) and Umbanda, and an increase in the number of people who say they have no religion at all.

Brazilian followers of Candomblé take part in a ceremony honouring one of their gods.

TRADITIONAL BELIEFS

Candomblé is a religion based on traditions brought to Brazil by African slaves, which integrated with elements of Catholicism. For example, it merges Roman Catholic saints and African deities, so that St. George is also Ogum, god of war and metals. The number of Candomblé followers has grown across Brazil in recent years as what was once seen as a lower-class religion has come to be valued as authentically Brazilian.

CARNIVAL!

The four-day pre-Lenten Carnival in Brazil shows the combination of a Roman Catholic holy festival with the lively celebrations of people of African ancestry. It is celebrated in every Brazilian city, but Rio's is the most famous and exuberant. Many people are involved in dancing, singing and making music, as well as constructing floats, making elaborate costumes and festooning the city with streamers and lights.

Over a million tourists join Brazilians at the annual Carnival in Rio for the biggest street party in the world!

33

SPORT AND LEISURE

A member of the children's samba school Estacio de Sa takes part in a rehearsal for the upcoming carnival in Rio.

MUSIC AND DANCE

Millions of Brazilians spend their leisure time learning how to dance the samba in preparation for Carnival. These samba schools also function as community clubs and neighbourhood centres where people can get together and have fun. Music inspired by Samba dance and jazzy Bossa nova music is popular in Brazil and around the world. However, as the country has developed, more and more people listen to rock music and some radio stations play mainly US hits.

BIG AND SMALL SCREENS

Today, about 90 per cent of Brazilian households have TV sets and Brazil has one of the largest television networks in the world. In cinemas, more than 60 per cent of films shown are from Hollywood, but the most popular TV shows are soap operas such as the highly popular *Avenida Brasil*, which is produced in Rio and set in the rich suburbs of that city. It is watched by an average of 46 million viewers each episode. A version of *Strictly Come Dancing* has also gathered a huge following in recent times, but it has a uniquely Brazilian flavour with more Latin and Caribbean dances than ballroom numbers.

FOOTBALL MAD

Football is played all over Brazil, watched avidly on TV and draws huge crowds to matches. In 2014, Brazil hosts the World Cup. The football association FIFA has agreed to increase the number of cities hosting World Cup matches in Brazil from the usual 10 to 12. This will give more Brazilians the chance to see a match and spreads the economic benefits of the event around the country. Brazil's second most popular sport is volleyball, often played on courts at the country's beaches, such as Rio's Copacabana and Ipanema beaches.

Beach volleyball is one of Brazil's most popular leisure activities.

MINI FOOTBALL

Futsal is an exciting five-a-side version of football played with a smaller ball on a smaller court that was developed in Brazil in the 1930s and 1940s, due to the lack of available football fields. Many schools teach futsal and many famous Brazilian soccer players such as Pelé, Ronaldo and Ronaldinho began their careers playing the sport.

FOCUS ON: RIO

A DAY TO REMEMBER

It was an historic moment. On 2 October 2009, Rio de Janeiro was named the host of the Summer Olympics in 2016. It was the first time a city in South America had been chosen to host the Games. Officials declared a holiday for city and state employees, and tens of thousands of people celebrated on Rio's streets and beaches. The Olympics are seen as a chance for Brazil to show the world its energy and vitality and the government plans to invest nearly £11 billion in infrastructure in preparation for 2016.

BUILDING UP

The investments in infrastructure for the games are also intended to benefit its people in the long term. Ahead of the Olympics a new tunnel is being blasted through a hillside to extend one of the city's two underground train lines, adding six more subway stations. The city has also invested in dozens of new buses which travel in exclusive lanes. This has cut the journey time to work by half for some of the city's poorest residents, and it is hoped that by 2016, 60 per cent of local people will use the new transport systems. The Olympic Park will be built on the former Brazilian Grand Prix track at Jacarepagaú and private developers will help to construct some of the new buildings such as a media centre and accommodation for the 20,000 foreign journalists who will cover the Games. After the Games, organisers plan to convert part of the park into South America's first Olympic Training Centre.

FAVELA FUTURE

The Rio Olympics are affecting the city's favelas. One favela, Vila Autodromo, is being threatened with demolition to make space for the Olympic Park. Favelas surrounding the Park area are being improved, not only with better lighting, but also with increasing numbers of community police stations. The safer, improved favelas are attracting property buyers because they have good views and hillside locations near the Olympic site, and owners will be able to rent out rooms at high prices to sports tourists during the Games. Property prices are rising as a result. Some poorer people are already being forced out of the improved favelas because they cannot afford rising rents which doubled from 2012 to 2013.

Brazilians celebrate the country's winning bid to host the 2016 Olympic Games.

BACKLASH

In the summer of 2013 there were huge demonstrations across Brazil against inequality, crime and the huge cost of hosting the World Cup and the Olympics. Millions of protestors demanded that the government invest more in public services, such as education, policing and healthcare, that genuinely helped people in Brazil.

The main construction zones for the 2016 Summer Olympics in Rio.

'It's not like we're going to be perfect by the end of the Games. Brazil still has a long way to go, Rio still has a long way to go, but it is going to be a more equal, more just, more integrated city after the Games. Bringing the Games here will mean the gathering of nations, of sports - what it always means - but it will mean lots of change for a great country and a great city.'

Eduardo Paes, mayor of Rio de Janeiro

DEODORO

Vigario Geral

■ INTERNATIONAL AIRPORT

MARACANÃ

Guanabara Bay

Complexo do Aemão ●

RIO NITERÓI BRIDGE

PORT

MARACANÃ STADIUM ■

■ SANTOS DUMONT AIRPORT

PEDRA BRANCA NATIONAL PARK

COPACABANA

RIO DE JANEIRO

Cidade de Deus ●

CHRIST THE REDEEMER

SUGAR LOAF MT. ▲

TIJUCA NATIONAL PARK

■ OLYMPIC VILLAGE

LAGOA RODRIGO DE FREITAS

COPACABANA

IPANEMA

BARRA DA TIJUCA

● PLANNED OLYMPIC ZONES

■ BUILT-UP AREAS

■ FAVELAS

BARRA   *Atlantic Ocean*

SOURCING ENERGY

Energy is vital for development. It provides power for everything from running machines and lorries to lighting up schools. The problem is that most energy is generated by burning fossil fuels such as oil, natural gas and coal. Some of the gases released by burning fossil fuels can cause air pollution, leading to asthma, breathing difficulties and even serious illnesses. Other gases released collect in the atmosphere, trapping the Sun's heat, leading to rising temperatures and changing weather on Earth. Most developed countries, including Brazil, are trying to produce more of their power sustainably to slow global warming and because supplies of oil, coal and natural gas are gradually running out.

Brazil's giant Itaipu hydroelectric dam on the Paraná River generates 20 per cent of all the country's electricity.

WATER SHORTAGE

Brazil makes about two-thirds of its power in hydroelectric power stations. This is a sustainable energy source which harnesses the energy of moving water in its rivers. However, in 2013 poor rainfall led to a hydroelectricty shortage. The government wanted to avoid rationing electricity because this had negatively affected development in the past: eight months of rationing in the Northeast in 2001 had resulted in losses to industry of approximately US$26 billion. Instead, it imported expensive gas from neighbouring Bolivia. As a result, Brazil now is sourcing more of its own gas resources for times of hydroelectricity shortage, an unfortunate situation that is likely to be more common as global warming changes rainfall patterns.

BIOFUEL

Brazil first started using sugar from its cane plantations to make ethanol as fuel for vehicles in the 1970s, when oil was expensive to import. Since then it has developed a big biofuel industry. Most cars in Brazil can use ethanol or petrol and much of the fuel sold at pumps is a mixture of the two. From 2014 a new way of extracting the ethanol will be used, meaning that the waste cane will also produce ethanol. As a result, every field of sugar cane will yield over a third more ethanol than before, making biofuel cheaper and more abundant. As Brazil develops and more people can afford cars, demand for fuel will increase. The country hopes its biofuel can increasingly meet this demand.

Since 2003, Brazil's use of ethanol fuel has reduced its emissions of carbon dioxide by 128 million tonnes.

39

THE AMAZON

Deforestation threatens a wide range of plants and animals, making some, like these wild hyacinth macaws, an endangered species.

AMAZON RICHES

The enormous Amazon rainforest is a wonderful natural resource of valuable trees, land and hidden minerals. Over the years trees have been cut down to access these resources, to clear land for roads, mines and farms, or to use the trees themselves.

LAND USE

The government has encouraged some deforestation. In the 1970s it gave areas of forest to landless people to convert to farmland, and in 2013 it subsidised the massive Belo Monte hydroelectric dam which was built partly on deforested land to supply regional power. Most deforestation is now illegal and is carried out by poor settlers or rich landowners. An area of forest twice the size of the whole UK was cleared between 1970 and 2010.

IMPACTS

Deforestation removes both tribal lands and animal habitats. Farmers clearing forest sell on valuable tree logs, but burn the rest. This releases carbon dioxide, as does the cleared soil, which can also wash into and clog rivers. Trees absorb carbon dioxide to make their food, so fewer trees means more greenhouse gases in the atmosphere, which contributes to global warming. Forest trees also suck up water through their roots and release water vapour into the atmosphere, creating rain, so deforestation is reducing rainfall in the Amazon and even drying up some rivers. In fact, atmosphere changes in the Amazon are so great that they disrupt normal rainfall patterns in Mexico and the USA.

SLOWING DEFORESTATION

Between 2004 and 2011, 57 per cent less carbon dioxide was released due to Amazon deforestation than in previous years. The Brazilian government has learned to protect its rainforest better. It uses satellites to monitor forest loss and fines illegal cattle ranchers and loggers it discovers. Deforestation reduction has been so successful that the government may now change its rules about forest protection. In the past farmers and ranchers could only cut down trees from a maximum of 20 per cent of their land, but many politicians felt these restrictions were hampering agricultural development and voted to relax deforestation rules. President Rousseff is preventing the law change as she pledged on election to reduce deforestation by 80 per cent by 2020, but she faces continued opposition as development in the Amazon region is seen to be crucial to the growth of the Brazilian economy.

Pristine tropical rainforest is still being cleared for activities such as cattle ranching.

Tree seedlings such as these are being used to reforest some deforested areas of the Amazon rainforest in Brazil.

41

THE FUTURE

WORLD POWER

Brazil is developing fast and playing an increasingly important role in world affairs. It is on the verge of becoming a permanent member of the powerful United Nations Security Council, which maintains world peace and security. Through booming exports and government programmes, the country has raised the living standards of millions of Brazilians. However, 20 per cent of the population still lives in poverty and it needs to do more to help these people, including investing in infrastructure such as roads and communications, and improving education. Education and careful policing can also help to reduce crime and other social problems, especially in the favelas.

Members of the Kayapo, an indigenous Amazon tribe known worldwide for their struggle to preserve the rainforest, protest at the Rio+20 Earth Summit (see box).

RIO+20

The first Earth Summit was held in Rio in June 1992. In 2012, a second Rio conference focused on how sustainable development could bring more people out of poverty. Critics said the agreement reached during the conference included little real detail on how this would be achieved. At a time of economic slowdown, few developed nations wanted to commit much money to help developing nations become more sustainable. Indigenous people also protested against the stripping away of indigenous people's land rights and what they described as the 'financialisation' of nature.

CHALLENGES OF DEVELOPMENT

Increasing wealth from recent oil discoveries should help to fund Brazil's development goals, but the country must be careful to develop its oil fields in ways that benefit the country over a long period of time without polluting its marine and coastal environment. The other problem with oil is that it is non-sustainable. In order to improve Brazil's energy sustainability, it needs to follow through on projects such as building 60 large dams in the water-abundant Amazon to power the country, and increase production of biofuels. But these plans need to be achieved by balancing the needs of the environment and the local people who may be affected by such projects with the drive for economic development. Brazil is rich in many ways – geographically, in resources, people, culture and biodiversity. With careful governance and commitment to sustainability, the country has a future to look forward to with optimism, and an important role to play in global affairs.

Brazil's children and the country they live in should be on the path to a bright future.

GLOSSARY

anaconda a huge non-venomous snake.

biofuel natural alternative to fossil fuels obtained from plant or animal materials.

BRICS stands for Brazil, Russia, India, China and South Africa, countries that are all deemed to be at a similar stage of newly advanced economic development.

capybara a large rodent.

colony settlement formed by a group of people in a place that is not their original home.

commodities materials or products that can be bought and sold.

democracy country governed by people who are elected by its citizens to make decisions on their behalf.

dissenter person who refuses to follow or belong to the established authority.

drought long period of time with little or no rain.

export to sell goods or services to another country.

favela area of poor, low-quality housing in Brazil.

favelado someone who lives in a favela.

fossil fuel fuel such as oil, gas or coal formed from the remains of plants and animals.

GDP stands for Gross Domestic Product; total value of goods and services produced by a nation's economy in a year.

global warming increase in the average temperature of the Earth's atmosphere.

greenhouse gas gas that traps heat in the atmosphere.

hemisphere half of the Earth, usually as divided into northern and southern hemispheres by the Equator.

hydroelectric using the power of water to generate electricity.

IMF International Monetary Fund; a United Nations agency that promotes trade by overseeing the global financial system.

import to buy goods or services from another country.

indigenous belonging naturally to a region or country.

infant mortality death rate of children less than one year old.

infrastructure public facilities and services, such as highways, bridges, schools, and sewer and water systems.

migrants people who move from one country or region to another.

military dictatorship a form of government controlled and enforced by the military.

natural resources materials found in nature that are used by people.

plantation huge farm where crops such as tobacco, sugar or coffee are grown.

Protestant someone who follows a branch of Christianity that is not Roman Catholic or Orthodox.

rainforest hot, humid forest found near the Equator.

refineries factories that convert oil to fuels.

sanitation measures for hygiene, such as sewage and waste disposal.

satellite equipment that orbits the Earth that is used for information or communication.

subsidise to give financial support.

sustainability using or managing sources (such as fuels) in a way that ensures they won't run out.

Transatlantic slave trade the selling of African slaves across the Atlantic Ocean between Europe and the Americas.

tributary river or stream that flows into a bigger river.

United Nations (UN) international organisation of countries set up in 1945 to promote international peace, security and cooperation.

urban migration movement of people from the countryside to cities.

water vapour water in the form of a gas in the air.

wetland low area of land saturated (soaked) with water, such as a marsh or swamp.

FURTHER INFORMATION

BOOKS

Brazil (Countries around the World) Marion Morrison (Raintree, 2012)

Brazil (Unpacked!) Susie Brooks (Wayland, 2013)

Brazil (Countries in Our World) Edward Parker (Franklin Watts, 2012)

The Real Brazil Daniela de Sousa (Franklin Watts, 2014)

WEBSITES

http://www.guardian.co.uk/the-report/riodejaneiro
Discover more in-depth information about Rio de Janeiro and Brazil, including sustainable development, dealing with housing crisis and more.

http://www.bbc.co.uk/news/world-latin-america-11413590
Young peoples' educational opportunities differ widely in Brazil. Find out more, including videos of what schools there can be like.

http://www.olympic.org/rio-2016-summer-olympics
Find out the latest information about the Rio Olympics, from planned events to development of infrastructure, to its legacy.

https://www.cia.gov/library/publications/the-world-factbook/geos/br.html
Full of solid, factual information and statistics about Brazil.

http://www.fifa.com/worldcup/index.html
The official website of the 2014 World Cup in Brazil. Full of news, photos and videos.

INDEX